Vinpoemlyri

–CVENSWRITES

Poetry and thoughts

Content

----

1. Gospel of the sinner....
2. Ink of cvens....
3. Actual truth about Life in terms of success.
4. Rainy cold....
5. Morning sky....
6. With time to fade away....
7. Her white gown....
8. Lying love.....
9. Walking days...
10. Little bird....
11. The short trees....
12. Beautiful hell....
13. The mingle and the influence....
14. Sudden 7.....
15. Five Paradox Stanza Of-cvenswrites.....
16. Just five of-cvenswrites quotes....
17. Spared joy.....
18. Stormed (a)live....
19. Question to ONESELF....
20. Night with a friend....
21. Thoughts.

◗CVENSWRITES

Gospel of the sinner...

Am a sinner...
Still scared of hell ..
I hope God forgives ,
So I don't get sinked by my sin

I'm still of flesh and blood
Going through moods of happiness,
sadness, depression, confusion and
all associate.

The moon knows my sins
and the sky witness my every mood..
Please save me that I may be safe to
see another sky in all her moods...

I hope before death to
die righteous and not of the
Im morals....

Oh' save my soul.

-cvenswrites 🍀

Ink of cvens(1)

❀ ❀ ❀ ❀ ❀

You can't regain a trust when it's
broken...
So don't break it!
You can't eraze words already said...
So mind how you speak!
We don't heal when we are broken,we
just get used to it...
So please don't break hearts!
We learn just by failing...
So don't condemn anyone!
That we are poor today doesn't
mean we will never be rich...
So don't look down at anyone!
We are one human living in this planet
Earth, because it's a residual home for us...
So don't be a racist!

-cvenswrites ❀

Actual truth about life in terms of sucess

.There are those it took years for them to get there.

.There are those who made it without much struggle.

.There are those who made it easily because of their
connections.

.There are those who made it but had to
go extreme,of doing more than just enough.

.There are those who made it because of there
social class.

.There are those who didn't struggle much to get
there..because luck found them...

.Yet, there are still those who keep the hustle tight and
choose to believe that they would be there someday
...even though no one has yet seen their value...

There are those who has done more than enough to
be qualified in getting there someday but still struggling

*...May be life is indeed **Unfair***
and no man's finger is ever equal to the other...

it may work for the other in a certain way but
wouldn't be so for you..

-cvenswrites ❀

<del>Rainy cold</del>

It's getting dark and
the rain takes no pity
but to shower the feet
Of it's soil.

To my thoughts I hope it wasn't going to be
much but that was
a lie to my own knowledge.. because
outside it's already flooded by it's
cold, causing fogs liquid and ice
to surround my sight and it's coldness to
my breath.

Thunder speaks in harshness
cutting the ribs covered by my skin
But made a slight wound to my heart
when it speakth of demand...

Demand that I must stay up
Demand that I must watch
Demand that I can't sleep till
secure my house hold in other
to avoid it's harshness to strike and
direct the sky tears to fill up my doors
without knocking..

I am scared and freezed to
my blanket, **"shivering"**
but my eyes remains unclosed
until veryily am sure the rain calms
Not to yell by her rumbles but to
leave a rainbow at my door so at
my first step out,.. I could see it once more".

-cvenswrites 🍀

Morning sky...

Too beautiful that I may still breath
Bluish and sometimes pure because
it's a new day..

It's breeze is as cold but fresh to be
noticed that the sky has been bathed
throughout the night for it's new appearance
today.

It seems void
But filled with smile that even
the birds sings to it in an early morning "twittering"
with a certain
melody..

The upper breath felt it the most
Because with there wings at least they can
fly up up there...

But to us standing to the land
From the down level we can raise up
with our eyes closed and takes in the fresh breath..

Indeed it's a new day.

-cvenswrites 🍀

-morning Everyone 🩶

With time to fade away...

It's soo white up there
Clearly that's the cloud..
It's covering everything up
there but we still act as if
it's really fine because we
got use to it...

Regardless we wanted to see
the blue beauty pasted to the sky
but maybe its just with time for the
Present cloud to fade away..

It makes no sound nor fades easily
but with time and our eyes fastened
to the sky...we can tell of it's kinetics....

This is how it feels likening our feeling to the
fading clouds...

We all have something we cheerish so much that
they are as beautiful as the clouds we don't mind
what they are really blocking from our lives...

And we wish they fade not...

But with time they did...
We sometimes noticed...
And sometimes we don't..
Because our eyes weren't fasten
Unto them..

-cvenswrites 🍀

Her white gown ()

Light blues on the lips of the sky
White cloud surrounded her body
and in her lies the Celestia body
With just the moon and sun popping
Up at it's time to shine..

Truly she cares not just for me
but the whole humanity, some who
threaten to hurt her...

But after her yell that may be as harsh as the
thunder bolt sounds
or her tears that's like the rain...

She leaves a rainbow up there for
us proving she's sorry to all and forever
her love remain constant 🩶

-cvenswrites 🍀

Lying love...

Love from heart was what
I thought but then guess it
was only it's disguised for am
Blinded falling for it not knowing
it came for an advantage without
an understanding...

So much is true, but blinded by
my eyes probably I couldn't see...

Things are easy said lying to ones
heart and filling it up with toxic fake tears...

Drowning in your lies
I wanna wake up it sounds

But just to find out it's hard
to go back to the real reality
And hurt, bruised by your lies
and so as everything that's around.

My heart's changed by the stain
Of current love blinding me of
what truly love means ...

But someday am gonna wake up
from this dirty lying dreams and to
my self I do promise never to look
back!

-cvenswrites 🍀

Walking Days..

It's just yesterday, we
were all born. Sleep to
bed in mum's arm till
we learn how to find our
own bed.

In each day is a role we have
to play whether it's ugly, or fine
our role in each day decides just
to come by the end of the day to
have us thinking.

In our 7's, our parents wish becomes
our ambition
In our 10's to 14's, we have a wish of our
own base on what inspired us and what's
surrounds us.

But in our 18's, we come to realize that we have so
much to work for because those wishes have no
magic in them to automatically appear as desired
to our hearts....

And while the age rise up, the role
keeps on speeding up because perhaps
that's how it's meant to be...

But who knows...
Maybe it's just how we are called for.

-cvenswrites 🍀

Little bird...

Little bird stay up
stay high, please stay
with me.

I know your wings are spreadable
and in a blink you can be seen no
more because to the furthest you
can reach.

Little bird Twitter's, chirps, yet
Sing and lose not your voice nor
your melody because deep it can
sink ye, in to my heart...
Reminding me of things lost.

Little bird...
Stay good, stay up until
you see I could fit in to your
wings.. maybe together we could
fly..

-cvenswrites

The short trees.

Life is scary
Imagine the small tree
stay there and watch
but in the process of growth
died, some with uncompleted
parts and some still grow.

Life is scary,
Behold is a high mountain
that had to grow higher than
it's siblings who remain short
to be stepped and spit on.

Life is scary,
So many puzzles unsolved by
those who had to chew their fingers
for it to be solved but to those who were
born of silver plate sort out the puzzle in
few minutes.

... Tik tik tik...
The time is running by..

Isn't it scary?

-cvenswrites ☘

Beautiful hell

Deep it's itching in
Every ocean of my
Blood

Very very deep I know

I got not scared when those
Eyes gleam in the dark and laugh
at me with there fork tongue..

I fear not when I was touched by
Unseen faces ... Perhaps they are
faceless... But their tears stroll
Through my blood vein to make
me understand what they are going through..

Am surrounded by colorless space
Nither dark nor white but sure I am
there's a blazing fire...

It tickles for a moment and aches in 10 minutes
before it dissolves...
But at it dissolve I feel not pain, no emotions
but at a state of total calm ...

Calm that my hand I feel not
My legs I feel not
My heart I feel not
Tears are gone
And emotions to feel is faded.

This the pain I felt
Through the hell

And so to my memories I remembered
if I was alive...
Certainly I will feel all that went
lost in the doom place I place my
being...

Perhaps the real hell is among humanity...
It's living among the living right now
Because that's set to be so....

But then there after being alive
Could be the calm. It feels like being
Placed on wools but colorless, yet
Spacious is the environment.....

.There lies the beautiful hell...

-cvenswrites 🍀

The mingle and the influence...

Mingle with the kind of people you
want to become for yourself, cause

If you mingle with a criminal
You will definitely become a criminal

If you mingle with positive mindset people
You will start to become more optimistic
in most things.

If you mingle with people with ambition
You will definitely start to think like them.

If you mingle with toxic people
You will definitely lose yourself someday.

All because human are more attached to
behave like what is more closer to them.

-cvenswrites 🍀

Sad weather...

Why you cry so much
More with your tears filled
On the floor..

I know the beat
I heard the wipe
I know the thunder strike
on multiple beats just on you
That you went cold without showing us the smile.

Not until 3pm
Before you could smile for a while
But short period of time before you
take off your smile..

Am sorry your day is over shadowed
By sad grieve even not your smile could
stay longer...

Am sorry but am concerned
Because to me that lives beneath you
It hurts to my heart without a joy but
worries I swim in ... Why you had to cry
as much as you did...

I wonder if you could still smile
Onces more to me for the night..
Or perhaps would you put on fake
Smiles just to give me uncertain
feeling that wouldn't grieve along
Your side...

Ohh dear
How I wish onces more you
Could smile so I can see the
Moon light that's beneath you
When you are empowered with
Joy over load...

-cvenswrites

sudden 7

I don't wanna die
But the prophecy of death
is once again brought to my heart
Knocking...

Looking at the moon
And it's beauty I just
Don't wanna stop seeing
The moon and the nature around

You know,...

. . .

-cvenswrites 🍀

five paradox stanzas
of -cvenswrites

There's no **hero** without a **villian**
There's no **winner** without a **competition**
There's no **life** without **struggle**

There's no **agreement** without **negotiation**
There's no **good** without **challenging moments**
There's no **over coming** without **temptation**

There's no **apology** without **confrontation**
There's no **darkness** without **a tunnel end point**
There's no **hell** without **saviour**

There's no **getting better** without **critics**
There's no **life** without **death**
There's no **fearless** without **danger**

There's no **bravery** without **war**
There's no **wisdom** without **tricks**
There's no **happiness** without **bitterness**

For only those who face through the opposite
side would value and understand it's other
beautiful side.

-cvenswrites 🍀

Just five of
-cvenswrites quotes...

No matter whatever it is
Human or not, don't let it
Stop your good wishes and
Ambition.

Believe it or not
You may not know the end
But to get to a point in your life
Is up to you and whatever you do now.

99% of love is just a fantasy
But just 1% which can be true
Is enough to cover up those 99%

(But it's still a fantasy and up to you to do the calculation)

Love is a **fantasy**
Hatred is the **reality**
Mixture of those is the **society**

If you don't use your sense
You will end up alone
Fight for what deserve it
And just glance **over** the ones that doesn't

-cvenswrites

❁ ❁ SPARED JOY ❁ ❁

It's true said of the things we had before,
those happy time, positive
Feeling, and optimistic conversation

It's all beautiful and the response
From you still makes it shiny...

We've made a memory and always
we will still miss those moments of
laughter, hope, sadness, moody and
Joy...

It's still the best part that
We never got disconnected
We saved the spared joy 🤍

-cvenswrites 🍀

Stormed (a)live...

Dark in I fall,
Dark in I rise...

Before and after birth
Love is seized from my home,
heart and knowing...
Smile is found pasted on my face
but not in my heart.

For inside my heart is darken and
burnt by the sands am stepping on..
But those smile are just there pasted
on my face so that I can live more
longer for sadden face may get be dead in hell...

I never know love but start losing
those important to me it cracked
more of me but no matter what you
will never see me cry...

Because the world taught me
there's no sympathy to the tears of
a man...

Breath I lost, breath I regain
Tears I cried, tears I dried
Wound I feel, wound I heal
Pain I met, pain I embrace

Until pain taught me to smile,

Dizzy caught me , and suicide
chopped me till I could open up
my retina in the hospital bed...

Souls yell at me as the devil knocked
to my heart feeding my soul with ugly
feeds, and only to that I could see knowing it's
stabbing my bones to the ground..

But in all of these shadows
It took 3-67 days multiple 2+
To regain my soul, body and blood...
For hope walked to my rescue
and even though it sometime fades
I could still smile for along the
pages of my lifetime,
I met hope.

-cvenswrites 🍀

Question to ONESELF....

I wish I had known it would be
this way , I wouldn't have taken
the red path for it was first disguised
as a way out, for it reads with feeling

So I thought as I felt...

If I regret, I don't know
If I never regret, I don't know
But I just wonder what my life
Could have been like if I had follow
The other way round...

Where could I have been...
Could I still meet you?
Could I still meet them?
Could things turn out this way?

Maybe I could have made more friends or
Maybe I wouldn't be exposed to the outside world..

Because my world is filled with sorrow and
slangs and sordids
May still have more to cry upon...

Or maybe I could be off this world and have no
pen-ink to bleed on from which cometh from my
heart...

Till now.. I still wanna know
If I could see the other way round...
If I could actually be happy through
this path I have choosen...

So save my soul
Dear lord as so
Saveth the over thinker...

-cvenswrites ☘

NIGHT WITH A FRIEND. 🍀

We use to be good, and shared
every memories and to be accepted
regardless of my different kind..
You accepted me.

Closer we became
Happier we felt and
before danger you saved me.

But years past and I waited
for your response but I understand
the pain you felt for my presence in
your life, between you and your other
soul went deep cutting veins.

And in once upon a time in a night
when I failed to capture my own self
we meet again... Exchanging feeling
and promising to be allies.

"Nakamada" 😊

My lost smile I could barely put on
Because the one night faded not
completely in my heart... With just
talk and positive thoughts...

I just want to let you know
That once upon a time in a night
Made me smile.

-cvenswrites 

Thoughts

Thought will warn you.
Thought will destroy you.
Thought will calm you.
Thought will amend you.
Thought will make you bad.
Thought will make you good.

But thought can't make decisions for
you.... Just that, it will be up to you to
fulfill whatever picture that your thoughts
has depicted to your mind.

-cvenswrites 🍀

Contact:

Email : vincentcven24@gmail.com

 Vinpoemlyri